HOW TO
REALLY
STINK AT
WORK

NAME

HOW TO
REALLY
STINK AT
WORK

A Guide to Making Yourself Fire-Proof
While Having the Most Fun Possible

Jeff Foxworthy
& Brian Hartt

Illustrations by
Layron DeJarnette

VILLARD Ⓥ NEW YORK

Published in the United States by Villard Books, an imprint of
The Random House Publishing Group, a division of
Random House, Inc., New York.

VILLARD BOOKS and VILLARD & "V" CIRCLED Design are
registered trademarks of Random House, Inc.

ISBN 978-0-345-50280-3
eBook ISBN 978-0-345-51534-6

Printed in the United States of America on acid-free paper

www.villard.com

2 4 6 8 9 7 5 3 1

First Edition

Book design by Susan Turner

PREFACE

Perhaps you find the title of this book puzzling. Why on earth would anyone want to stink at his or her job? Think about it: We all stink at something, and I would much rather it be my job than sports or sex.

The opposite of stinking at your job is being really good at it, and that is where the trouble begins. Being really good at your job probably means you'll be promoted, which means increased responsibility. Are you going to let a bigger salary bribe you into being responsible? I didn't think so!

Besides, increased responsibility means longer hours. Shouldn't you want to work less? Isn't that what life is all about? After all, nobody on their deathbed says, "I wish I had spent more time at the office."

Holding an important job means being accountable to management and possibly even stockholders. Who can have any fun with that kind of anvil hanging over your head?

If you follow our simple guidelines, you will probably never make very much money and you'll greatly disappoint your parents and spouse, but you'll also eliminate a ton of work-related stress, which means you'll live a very long time without very much money. The semi-rotten apple is yours for the taking.

CONTENTS

HOW TO
REALLY
STINK AT
WORK

"STAY!"

THE JOB INTERVIEW

Before you can stink at your job, you have to secure a job. This process usually begins with the job interview. This is very important! Try to appear as normal and grounded as possible, at least for the interview. Smile a lot. You're trying to sell a product.

As you prepare your résumé, let the sky be the limit. Why waste years and a fortune actually getting a PhD at Harvard when you can just *say* you did? Employers like to hire people who have experience in their chosen field, so tell them what they want to hear. *Just get the job.*

To make yourself even more attractive as a potential employee, it is wise to "spice up" the personal/special skills part of your résumé.

Claim to have served in the Peace Corps, say you can drive an excavator and, incidentally, that you climbed Mount Kilimanjaro (twice). . . . Sounds good, right? Very impressive? Don't stop now—you're on a roll!

Tell them you have a black belt, play classical violin, and can speak *four* languages. Name it and claim it! They will be excited about having you on board . . . for now.

TIP: Do a good job of selling yourself, but try not to go too far. Telling the company that if they don't hire you they're stupid may backfire.

MAKE YOURSELF FIRE-PROOF

Now that you have the job, the real challenge begins. You have to give your bosses a reason *not* to fire you. One method is to do your job so well and with such enthusiasm that they would never dream of letting you go. Don't get caught in that trap.

The other option is to make it more of a mind game. Make them believe that you would not hesitate to bring a lawsuit against them. In fact, mentioning people you have sued and settlements you have won will create a buzz in management that will only help you down the road. From where the bosses sit, still having to deal with someone years after they've been fired doesn't make anyone's Monday mornings any easier.

As you weigh this decision, don't forget that the third option is to work really hard.

Every day.

For years and years and years and years.

You have to create a foundation that will make you unfireable for as long as you choose to remain there. Which, in effect, makes *you* the *boss*!

Now is the time to convince management that you are unstable. This, my friend, is the key to job security.

TIP: Naked pictures of your boss are a dandy "ace in the hole." Naked pictures of you *and* your boss—even better. Ahhhh, the magic of Photoshop.

PLANT THE SEEDS OF INSTABILITY.

CREATING THE ILLUSION

One way to become unfireable is to appear to have a serious injury or life-threatening illness. Firing someone in that condition is just begging for a lawsuit and/or bad publicity. If you weren't blessed with a medical condition, you will have to create the illusion that you were. Use their fear to your advantage. Here are a few ways to get started:

- When asked where you are going on vacation, meekly reply, "The Mayo Clinic."
- Purchase the largest pillbox you can find and fill it with Skittles. Make a big production of going to the water fountain every half hour or so to take your

"medication." No one with an ounce of decency would ask such an obviously sick person to do anything extra. Just the fact that you are "trying to work" creates sympathy and pushes others ahead of you in the firing line.

- A neck brace, plain and simple, is money well spent. It alludes to a serious injury that can get worse at any time. And because it's so hard and "painful" to turn your head, no one will call your name to ask you to do anything. All for the amazing low price of $39.95! You may also want to suggest that the neck brace is the result of your slip in the break room. The truth? No. Security? Absolutely.

- Another bonus of the neck brace is that it will make people avoid you, guaranteed! First of all, nobody wants to open Pandora's box by asking, "What happened?" (Caution: Have a spectacular story ready just in case— i.e., you fell off a nine-story building, you were hit by a train, a meteor fell on your house, etc., etc.)

- Also remember: Nobody wants to hang out with someone who's wearing a neck brace, and isn't that what you really want? Just to be left alone? As a birth control device, nothing may be more effective than a neck brace.

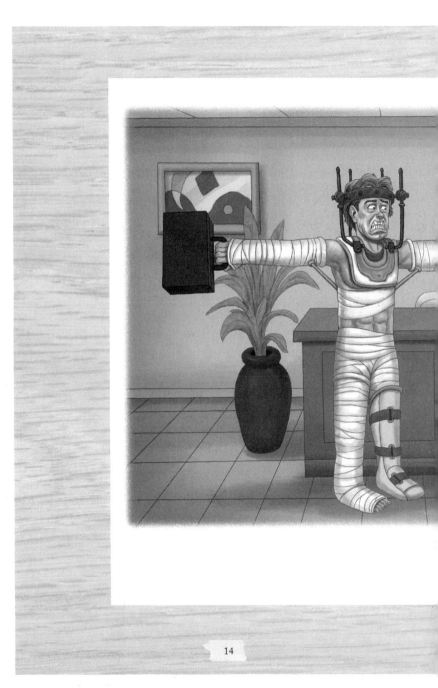

"So, how was **YOUR** weekend, Carol?"

SOMETIMES YOU FEEL
LIKE A NUT

If the physical-illness deception doesn't appeal to you, maybe you are more cut out for the "nut" route. Don't worry—it's just as effective. People, especially bosses, don't like weirdos. You don't have to be one; you just have to create the illusion.

If this sounds like your cup of tea, here are a few suggestions to help get you started:

- Wear a parka and a stocking cap to work every day. Even in the summertime. If possible, leave them on all day.

- On your desk, display at least five restraining orders and a framed picture of

you kissing a boa constrictor. Make sure
they are visible to anybody and everybody.

- Make up your own religion. If it involves
intergalactic travel, all the better. Who
knows—if they buy it, you just might get a
few religious holidays not listed in the
company manual.

Tip: Try putting up one of those
motion-activated wall hangers—
like that loud laughing skull they
sell at Halloween that goes off
when you walk past it. It will keep
people from wanting to come and
talk to you. About anything.

One way to keep people on their toes is to
bring a video camera to work. But don't ask any
questions or seem like you have any purpose
other than just recording everyone all the time.

"I'm just getting a cup of water."

GILDING THE LILY

Just to make yourself a little more unfire-able, proudly display a picture of you and the CEO of the company on vacation to-gether. Photoshopping makes this a snap. Your possible close relationship with the "big cheese" will make your boss think twice about cutting you loose.

And . . .

How would you like to have all kinds of different people write about how great you are at your job? Well, if your workplace has customer-comment cards, you can! And you don't have to wait for other people to do it. A change of pens and a slight alteration of hand-writing and you can pop off five or six of these glowing reviews by yourself. And just so it's not all about you, these "customers" can also make *you* look good by writing "personal horror stories" about how bad your co-workers are at their jobs.

TIP: Don't overdo it. Resist the temptation to include how "insanely hot" you are on every comment card. And proofreading is advised. Using "I" or "me" juuuuuust might send up a red flag.

"THAT WAS DON FROM HEADQUARTERS ASKING ME TO BE THE GODFATHER OF ANOTHER ONE OF HIS KIDS!"

REDIRECTING
THE SPOTLIGHT

Once you've made the commitment to be successful at not being successful, the real work begins. Doing nothing and getting paid for it is bound to draw attention, and that is something you don't want. You must learn to redirect the spotlight off yourself and onto others so that it's not obvious that you aren't doing crap all day long.

One way to do this is to casually mention to a co-worker that you saw his or her spouse arm in arm with "someone" while you were at lunch. Their anger (or tears) will cause others to move to comfort them, distracting everybody long enough for you to get in a couple of games of computer solitaire.

Stirring the pot can be subtle or obvious—just as long as it's stirred. A subtle tactic could be as simple as letting it slip that you heard that Betty got a nice raise last week. (Note: This works only if Betty is clueless.) Just by throwing that little "tidbit" out there, you can enjoy watching the entire office unravel. Things can be running as smooth as silk until someone catches wind that someone else is making more money for less work—then all hell breaks loose. Well done, my friend, well done.

Create a petition to have the boss fired, then go to the boss and tell him you just found it on your desk. Now sit back and enjoy the show. Nothing takes the focus off what you are or aren't doing like officewide mistrust.

Any time you see your boss walk out of his office, call his extension and let it ring until he walks back into his office; then hang up.

Without anyone knowing, change the time of a scheduled meeting . . . for everyone except you and the boss. You will be seen as responsible for being the only one there, and the meeting will get pushed back, hopefully forever.

TIP: If you throw out the rumor that someone is getting fired, everyone else will work way harder for the next few weeks, which means you can coast on the wave of their sweat.

Pick up reports and other important-looking papers from one co-worker's desk and put them on someone else's desk. The same thing can be done with family photos. Or suggestive magazines.

IF IT LOOKS LIKE WORK...
(You Must Be Working, Right?)

If you look busy, nobody will question what you are doing. Remember, it takes a lot of work not to do any work.

Keep a spray bottle in your pocket or purse and spray your face when no one is looking to make it appear that you are working very hard. While you are at it, spray your armpits and neckline. This becomes doubly effective if your job involves no physical labor.

Cover your desk with boxes full of old files. Pull several files out and pretend to be studying them. Trust me, nobody is going to volunteer to help you with a job like that. The bonus is that if you can "read" with your head resting in your hands, you can grab a quick nap.

Leave cold cups of coffee and half-eaten snacks on your desk. This implies that you were too busy to finish them. Call your own phone and leave a message so the "new message" light is always blinking.

If you don't have any of the following items slipped between the pages of whatever you are supposed to be working on, you are not avoiding work seriously: a crossword or sudoku puzzle, printed-out articles about your favorite sports teams, a wrestling magazine, Oprah's magazine, a mirror in which to practice making faces, a Game Boy, or a ten-inch TV.

TIP: As soon as files are put in your in-box, immediately, without looking at them, move them over to your out-box.

Make copies. Lots of copies. It really doesn't matter what they are of—you will damn sure look busy. If your job requires that you actually have to make copies, do whatever it takes to shut the copier down. Then act really frustrated that you can't get your work done.

I NEED A BREAK!

From time to time everyone needs a break. Studies show that it's good for productivity. You just happen to need a lot more breaks than other people. How to do that creatively is where we come in.

Leave your car lights on every day. Eventually someone will come to tell you that your lights are on, and you can get out of ten minutes of work by going out to the parking lot to rectify the problem. Surely they wouldn't fire you for turning your car lights off?

Bring something stinky, like a can of sardines, to work and hide it under a co-worker's desk. The search for the source of the smell is sure to take fifteen to twenty minutes of time that you otherwise would have spent "working." You can extend this diversion by initiating a conversation with "What kind of person would do something like that?"

Take multiple smoking breaks, even if you don't smoke. If someone challenges you, put a cigarette in your mouth but never light it.

TIP: Rub your clothes with cigarette butts so you smell like a smoker.

Fake phone calls are always good. Just make sure that when you're "talking" into your phone you have it on vibrate so you're covered if you get a real call when the boss walks by.

"I'll come when I'm done, Mr. Dask. I'm in the middle
of an important private call."

I NEED ANOTHER BREAK

- Make a big deal about celebrating everyone's birthday. Think about it: Someone will have to go out and pick up a card and a cake (you). Someone will have to get everyone in the office to sign the card (you). If you should "accidentally" forget to buy candles, that's yet another trip to the store. Play your cards right and anybody's birthday is a day when you can proudly accomplish nothing.

- Suddenly start gagging. Be choking so badly that someone has to do the Heimlich maneuver on you. After they pump you a few times, spit the cap from a Sharpie across the room. You'll definitely require some recovery time after that. Take all the time you need.

- Once in a while, just randomly shout out from your desk, "I am finally finished! I need a break!" and take one. You've earned it! Whew!

- If a family member or old friend drops by, you can't be rude—you have to stop work to introduce them to everybody, right? And then you have to visit for a while, right? Unfortunately, waiting for a relative or friend to drop by may take forever, especially if your family hates you and you have no friends. But, hey. As long as no one at your job knows the person, anyone can play the part.

JUST ENOUGH

Sometimes you will have to do some actual work. It can't be avoided. But when you do accomplish something, make sure everyone knows about it. Stroll past the boss's office and give her a shout-out: "Just wanted to let you know the payroll sheets are done!"

Routinely ask for a raise. No one would ask for more money if they were just slacking off, would they?

Also, encourage some energetic new kid on the block to do your work for you (or as you refer to it, "I'm taking him under my wing"). He does all the work; you take all the credit.

TIP: Loudly, and often, berate fellow employees for slacking off. It will create the appearance that you're a hard worker.

"I need a grand-a-week bump. These out-of-office expenses are killing me."

EXCUSES, EXCUSES

If you are really committed to being a marginal employee, you are going to have to become proficient at making excuses. This is where a creative mind comes into play. Learning to trim a little off both ends of the workday is a must.

If you are late to work, "I got stuck in traffic" is the most overplayed card in the deck. But it's used so often for a good reason: It's hard to disprove. Spice up your story with phrases like "on fire" and "Life Flight helicopter."

Car trouble—an oldie but a goodie. Car trouble is a great excuse because it tends to make you a little sympathetic, and it is certainly plausible. After all, your boss knows your "work ethic." The idea that you may have driven for weeks with the "check engine" light on is not out of the realm of possibility.

This excuse can be strengthened if you are willing to take off your shirt or dress and wipe it around the motor a couple of times.

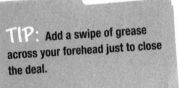

TIP: Add a swipe of grease across your forehead just to close the deal.

EXTRA TIP: If, for some reason, people are still skeptical, take a lighter to a bit of your hair. Who would burn their own hair?

"Sorry I'm late, class. Car trouble."

Here are some other excuses for your lack of productivity that won't draw too many questions:

- Urinary tract infection: You can enhance this one by moaning loudly (or occasionally screaming) while relieving yourself in the company restroom.

- Mammogram: Not likely to draw questions, provided you're female.

- Cracked tooth: Stick a wad of cotton in your jaw and do your best Godfather imitation. Every time someone asks how you're doing, just close your eyes and shake your head.

- Fungus: Claim that you had an appointment with a toe fungus specialist. Changing your socks three times a day and making a big production of throwing them away in a centrally located trash can makes this lie a real player. Caution: It can get expensive if played too long.

- Upset stomach: "I ate some bad sausage"—enough said.

- Financial distress: Let it be known that you are late because you met with someone to try to get a consolidation loan. If other people think you need to borrow money, they will avoid you like the plague.

- Unsavory private matters: Bring in an inner tube and sit on it all day. If anyone gets brave enough to ask, "What's the deal with the inner tube?" simply reply, "I had some boils lanced." No further questions, Your Honor.

STRUT YOUR STUFF

Confidence is king. Act like you've got it going on and most people will assume you do. Never avoid management—in fact, seek out your higher-ups. Ask about their spouses and their kids. Hide in plain sight!

Speaking of strutting, history has shown us that many underqualified women have moved up the company ladder by "showing off their assets." In this day and age it's a sin that they feel like they need to do this. It's sexist.

That is why men should be doing the exact same thing. Wear extremely tight pants all the time. What's good for the goose is good for the gander. If you are "package"-challenged—stuff!

TIP: When stuffing, avoid anything that leaks, makes noises, or moves on its own.

"Here's a coffee for ya, boss. Three sugars.
Sweet, just like you."

DOGGING IT

Bringing your dog to work is sure to rub some folks the wrong way, especially those allergic to dogs. And even if everyone's all right with it, management won't enjoy people wasting time by focusing on the dog, not on work. In fact, because of these reasons, lots of companies have a rule against bringing in a dog. But I seriously doubt that any company has a rule about bringing your grandmother to work. Have her sit in a chair next to your desk; if anyone dares question you about it, give Grandma the signal to start coughing.

At some point loudly hang up your phone and say, "Something came up!" Tell people you have to leave for a few hours. But before you go, get a fellow employee to keep an eye on your grandma while you're gone. Hand him some soft food in case she gets hungry. And ask him to occasionally check to see if she needs changing. Now you're off to a movie!

"Thanks for helping out. Her health is so bad, I'm
scared she'll croak if I leave her alone."

BUTT KISSING

To stay out of the line of fire, it's always a good idea to suck up to the boss. Of course, always comment on how cute and talented his kids are, even if they look like escapees from the primate center. Compliment his clothes, even if you work in construction. These things are no-brainers.

But why not take it to the next level? What better way to get brownie points than to snitch?

Let the boss know who came back ten minutes late from lunch. Keep him aware of who is making personal phone calls on company time. If there is an affair going on in the office, make sure the boss knows all about it.

If you are lucky enough to have a paranoid

boss, he'll start noticing all these "treacherous" things on his own (along with a few others he creates in his own mind) and you can focus your time and effort on other ways of getting out of work.

Make your co-workers' lack of respect for the company look like an epidemic and offer to wear a wire. If you can turn half of your work-day into spying on people you work with . . . well, you're halfway there.

TIP: As an employment insurance policy, make sure your boss's boss is aware of everything your boss does that's not by the book.

Jerry: Hi, Annie. Remember when you said the boss was stupid?
Annie: No. When did I say that?
Jerry: All the time. Remember?
Annie: Leave me alone.
Jerry: So you're not denying it?
Annie: Why are you moving your shirt toward me?
Jerry: Yes or no? Our boss is stupid?
Annie: You're an idiot.
Jerry: Nice talking to you. Bye.

CUTTING
THE WORKDAY SHORT

A great way to leave work early is to set off the fire alarm whenever possible. Granted, this is a felony, but remember, most prisoners don't have to work. Just make sure that you do it after lunch, because lunch is your free time and there's no sense in giving *that* away. Even if they don't evacuate the building, the panic is sure to eat up at least another half hour. And in all the confusion, no one will notice that you've done an Elvis and left the building

Gas leak in the building. This is accomplished by, well, cutting the gas line in the building.

Here's another idea: A can of SpaghettiOs mixed with lemonade makes a wonderful fake vomit. Distribute it when no one is looking, and accompany the distribution with retching noises. Do it right, and you, my friend, have just played the Get Out of Jail Free card.

TIP: Where you put the fake vomit is important. Down the back of a snotty co-worker, onto the files you need for the presentation you're not ready for, or right into your computer. How are you supposed to work with a fried workstation?

KEEP THE DREAM A DREAM

If you've always dreamed of doing something, *not* going after that dream is a great way to stink at what you're doing right now. The less you are into your work, the more you will try to not do it.

Chasing a dream requires hard work and determination. Just knowing that means you are doomed. But take heart: Never going after something also means you'll never fail.

If you've dreamed of being a hairdresser, go into construction. If you want to sing professionally, seek employment in food services. Being dissatisfied when you pull into the parking lot in the morning is a perfect way to set the tone for a great day of accomplishing nothing.

Miss the dance and tell Lee Ann Womack to kiss your butt.

"He always wanted to work in a bakery."

THE FAMILY BUSINESS

If the family business is handed down to you, it can create problems. If the business has been successful, people are going to expect that to continue. That smells too much like work to me, and you must take action fast.

Change the name of the business immediately! In fact, let the new name in no way allude to what the company actually does. For instance, Carlyle's Funeral Home could become Sammy's Stuff Shop.

In one quick move you've ruined years of hard work building a name that countless customers know and trust and you've alienated everyone who cares about you.

Congratulations! You are now on your way

to slower days and not having to deal with all those annoying customers.

TIP: Turning the sign on and unlocking the door is just asking for trouble.

If possible, change the business altogether. Imagine how surprised the clientele will be to find out, after forty years of home cooking, that Martha's Family Restaurant has become a transgender strip joint.

If you don't change the name or the business, at least change the hours of operation.

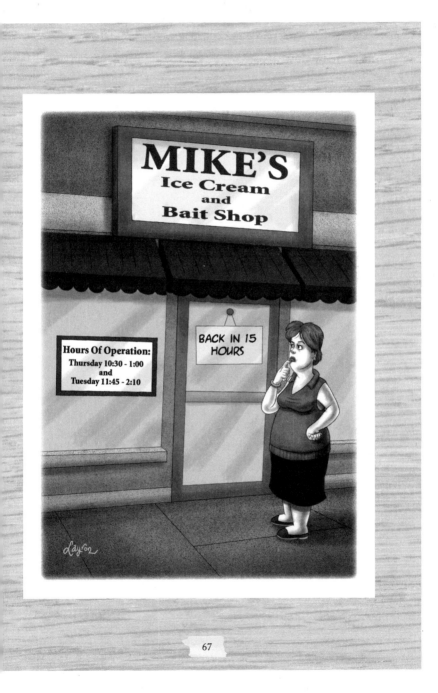

BE THE FUNNY GUY

This doesn't work if you are actually funny. People like to have funny people around, and that is not your goal. You want to be the "funny" person others turn and run from.

Here are a few ways you can be that person:

1. Try to have a witty comeback to everything anyone says. The first thing that comes to your mind, blurt it out. If you can't think of anything, just grab your crotch and simply insert what they were talking about into the phrase "I've got your (blank) right here."

2. Use a lot of old famous sayings as if you just made them up. When your boss asks you to do

something, throw out, "Whatchu talkin' 'bout, Willis?" Every time you get handed your weekly check, hold it as if you're weighing it and shout, "Where's the beef?" If the boss calls you into her office, scream, "Beam me up, Scotty!"

3. Always laugh at your own jokes. You'll need to let people know when you're being funny, because otherwise they won't have a clue.

4. Annoying practical jokes are a must. Shake up Bill's soda every other day. Hook all of Ellen's paper clips together. Forward every joke email to everyone in the office. Now you are definitely the not-funny guy.

5. Making a funny T-shirt is hard to do. Making an unfunny T-shirt that is offensive isn't. So fill your closet with "isn't."

MEETINGS

Most people hate meetings. They complain that they have too much work to do to spend time sitting in a meeting. That, *mi amigo,* is why *meetings are your friends.*

Whenever there's a meeting, make sure to have plenty of food around, even if you have to pay for it out of your own pocket. It is unlikely that anyone will pass up free grub, and as they feed their face the workday ticks away.

The most productive meetings are short, to the point, with an obvious purpose and goal. It's your job to make sure it doesn't go down this way. Come late, come loud, and come with an attitude. As you sit down, "accidentally" spill your coffee all over someone. Once the cleanup has been completed, talk way more than anybody else. Interrupt the presentation by asking lots of questions. It takes time to answer questions (wink, wink).

Keep stalling the meeting by trying to take a vote on everything. No matter what it is, don't let anything go by without a show of hands. If the boss says, "Let's hear from Jerry now," take a vote on whether or not Jerry should go next. If someone asks to open a window, take a vote on it. If people complain, pound your fist and ask, "Is this still America?!"

Take a side other than what is being presented and be very opinionated and emotional in your defense of it. If this doesn't appear to be working, lay your head down on the conference table and moan things like "Why can't we just do it the way we've always done it?! This sucks!"

Laughing out loud and making bizarre facial expressions are also good options.

If you do it right, there will be another meeting about whether you should be allowed to go to any more meetings. Of course you will not be in that meeting, and that is called nap time.

As a last resort, bring up things that have nothing to do with what you are meeting about. Try just randomly yelling, "How 'bout them Dawgs!" Then start barking and don't stop until you are forced to.

"Go Dawgs! Go Dawgs! Go Dawgs!..."

THE COMPANY BATHROOM

In more ways than one, the company bathroom is a great place to stink at work. No one is really comfortable in there anyway, so it is your obligation to turn it up a notch. After all, you have a reputation (as a nut) and you must protect it.

First of all, never, ever flush and never miss a chance to take care of a blackhead in the mirror. Let's give them something to talk about.

As you're killing part of a workday sitting in a stall, if you hear someone enter the restroom, get him or her to leave as quickly as possible. Here's how:

- Pretend to be on a cell phone talking to your significant other. Make it a personal, flirty call. One no one else should be listening to. Talk as sexy as you can about how hot the person you're talking to is and ask what they are wearing and what they are doing to themselves. Then proceed to say you are completely naked and completely turned on. You should hear the door close in a matter of seconds.

- Be amazed at something that just came out of you. "Holy cow!" and "You've got to be kidding me!" are good. Then shout out, asking if anybody has a tape measure and a camera. Again, you should hear the door close very soon.

- Sing a Christmas carol really loud. But don't do it near the holidays; it is much more effective from May to September. Every time you go to the bathroom, sing the same carol. Your co-workers will never listen to "Rudolph the Red-Nosed Reindeer" the same way again after you've grunted through a few hundred verses over the summer.

THE BREAK ROOM

This is a place to solidify your reputation as a whack job. Nobody wants to ask a crazy for help, and bosses sure don't want to fire them. This plays right into your hands. Here are some tips to help you find more "me time" at work:

- If your break room has a refrigerator, use it to your advantage. Fill a quart container with tomato juice, then write "goat's blood" and your name on a piece of tape and put it on the bottle.

- You can also put a paper bag with your name written on it in crayon in there. Mix equal parts sardines and Vienna sausages in a paper towel and place it in the bag. After a couple of weeks, remove the bag and offer some co-workers a taste.

- If the break room has a bulletin board, place an ad on it. Say you're looking for a guillotine, and offer live hand grenades as a possible swap.

- Never, ever eat with anybody else. Sit by yourself, even if it means on the floor in the corner. Loners never have to explain themselves.

- Occasionally eat someone else's lunch. But while eating it, complain about how crappy-tasting it is. Not only are you eating someone else's food, but you're complaining about it . . . *and still eating it!*

"Hey, Jerry! That lunch you left in here for a month has caught fire!"

ON THE ROAD

Your job may sometimes require you to travel. While this can offer a great opportunity for sightseeing, it is also perilously close to doing work. Remember that when you travel, you represent the entire company. Make your bosses question putting their valuable reputation in your hands. Here's how:

- Cover the outside of your briefcase with bumper stickers. Those advertising liquor, adult gift stores, and tobacco products are always good choices, as are pictures of illegal substances and people with very few clothes on.

- If you feel gaseous, don't try to contain it. Seriously, have you ever heard of someone getting fired for farting? Stepping on some dog poop, then tracking it into someone else's office building is also quite effective.

- Use makeup to create a black eye. If asked about it, just say, "It's in the hands of the Atlanta police now."

- Wear the same thing every day of your trip and don't wash or iron it. And be sure to wear bright colors like orange and purple so people remember the flashy, smelly guy.

- Buy a racy postcard, write on the back, "This place is crazy. Wish you were here!" and send it to the office.

- Collect every receipt you see while you are gone. A three-day trip with seventeen Burger King meals could create quite a large expense report. If Accounting has questions, explain that tapeworms run in your family.

"What do you make of this text I just got from Jerry in Orlando?"

THE COMPANY
CHRISTMAS PARTY

Most businesses have a company Christmas party, and it is a grand setting to distance yourself from the pack. Do it right and they'll be talking about it for years to come.

If there is a gift exchange, bring a box with holes poked into the top and drop crumbs in there during the course of the day. No one will dare select your gift and you'll be twenty bucks to the good.

Dress up an inflatable doll, place it in a chair in the corner, and introduce it as your date.

Comment on how "hot" your co-workers'

spouses are. It doesn't have to be true to be effective. Remember, your goal is to make yourself as unpromotable as possible.

TIP: If it's a Secret Santa gift exchange, make your present a two-pack of condoms. No matter where you work or whose name you draw, two condoms does not say "Merry Christmas" or "Happy Holidays."

I guarantee there will be a change in the mood when Bernice, the sixty-three-year-old temp, rips open her "surprise" and you say, "It's the first thing I thought of when I pulled your name out of the hat." It's a present that says so much, and none of it is complimentary.

"Wow! I'd do the sweat dance with her in a dumpster
next to a rendering plant! And I've got high standards."

LIE LIKE A RUG

As you've probably noticed, you are going to need to hone your skills at stretching the truth. But, really, what is a lie? It's simply the absence of truth, and that doesn't sound so bad, does it?

Now, the more you lie, the more lies you're going to have to remember. And it's unfair to expect you to remember them all. So if you get caught in a lie, just start sobbing and run to the bathroom. Overly emotional reactions make people uncomfortable, and they'll stop calling you out on your mistruths.

For example: When your *fourth* grandfather dies, people are going to start asking questions. Just remember: Burst into tears and peel off to your chosen "cry place." This will let everyone understand that *any* questioning of personal stuff comes with a maniacal outburst.

Hey! You may want to check out the bereavement policy at your workplace. Loss of an immediate family member often brings three days off, so the more brothers and sisters, the better. May they rest in peace.

TIP: If people think you lie all the time, they won't believe you even when you're telling the truth. So if this happens, tell the truth.

DIFFERENT OCCUPATIONS

Stinking at work can be customized to your chosen job. Here are some tips to make your workday far more interesting and much less productive.

RESTAURANT WORKER

People go to restaurants for good food and good service, and if they get it they might come back—or, worse, tell other people. That means more work for you. Yuck!

If your rating is higher than a "C," you are spending way too much time cleaning your restaurant and not enough time trying to figure out ways to get around cleaning it.

Five or six really loud sneezes before you

walk out of the kitchen is a nice touch. If you can't do a good fake sneeze, just yell, "Oh, gross!" People need something to worry about, so you are actually helping them.

When you are carrying drinks, make sure that your fingers are in them.

Occasionally stomp around on the floor like you're trying to kill a fast-moving bug.

Right before you take an overweight person's order, yell to the kitchen, "All hands on deck!"

RETAIL SALESPERSON

There are lots of places to buy stuff. Eliminate yours as one of the possibilities.

If a customer asks, "Does this come in my size?" try a witty reply like "I can't imagine that it would" or "If it does, I can't pick it up."

If you sell hearing aids, when discussing a customer's options quit talking audibly but keep moving your lips. They can't report you because they can't be sure if you are messing with them or not.

"How many menus would you like?"

When selling makeup, wait until a customer tries a new product. When they look at you for your opinion, start laughing. You can enhance this by yelling, "Happy Halloween!"

If you sell perfume, at a crucial point in the sale wave your hands in front of your face, take a step back, and suggest that the customer try using the fragrance inside her mouth.

DOCTOR

The last thing you need are patients. Patients = work. So how do we rid ourselves of these pesky people? Try this.

- Take the batteries out of your pager. This way you can concentrate on stinking at golf. (But you need to buy the book first.)

- Ask a patient what he thinks is wrong with him. However he answers, reply, "I see," then tell him, "I'll be right back." Leave for fifteen minutes (or however long it takes to check your email), then come back and say,

"This should cover up your old-lady smell."

"You might be right. Let's schedule surgery."

- Another effective way of clearing your appointments is to recommend totally inappropriate treatment. For instance, for a broken foot recommend that the patient gargle with salt water. A sore throat, on the other hand, might require a pacemaker.

TIP: For *any* operation, tell them you'll need to go in through the butt.

NURSE

Nurses are angels on earth. Their calm demeanor and strong constitution keep hospitals

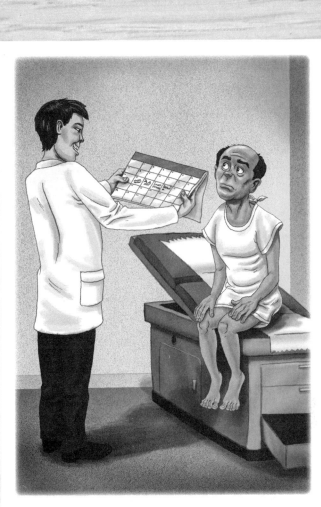

"I can't perform the operation on the 15th because I have anger-management class, the 16th I have AA, the 17th I'm in court, the 18th I am scheduled for the next session of my tattoo, so what about the 19th?"

and doctor's offices running smoothly. It's the nurse who has to deal with whiny patients and obnoxious family members.

Half of these people aren't badly hurt or really sick anyway and could treat themselves at home. A wooden spoon, some duct tape, and a little spunk is all you really need for a broken arm or neck.

So stay in the back and don't call their names for a really, really long time. After five or six hours, the only ones left in the waiting room will be the patients who truly need help.

Having trouble finding a patient's vein on, say, the first eight tries, while swearing a blue streak the whole time, can also empty a waiting room and create no return appointments.

GUTTER CLEANER

This is a dream-come-true job. It requires no effort on your part. Simply climb up on the roof and play a video game for a few hours. Then climb back down, tell the customer that you have cleaned their gutters, and collect your pay.

It's not like they are going to check. If they were going to pull out a ladder and climb up there, they would have cleaned their own gutters.

In fact, I bet it won't be long before they need their gutters cleaned again.

FOOTBALL REFEREE

Learning all the rules of football takes work, and isn't that what we're trying to avoid? Remember, you get paid by the game, not by the call. Blow the whistle to get the game started, then never blow it again. Not only do you make money, but you make it quick.

POSTAL WORKER

Don't drive yourself crazy sweating the little details, like names and addresses. Think about it: Misdelivered mail today means there will be a job for you tomorrow.

"You should be good to go."

JOE THE PLUMBER

You work by the hour, so the key to stinking at work is to do as little as possible for as long as possible. Take advantage of the fact that the customer probably has no idea how to fix the problem or she wouldn't have called you. Keep going back out to the truck for another tool (i.e., make a personal phone call or have a couple of smokes).

Make it appear that the problem is much more complicated than you originally thought. Go to the basement or attic a lot. Those are great places to check up on your fantasy football league.

You will learn to gauge when the customer is totally exasperated with having you in their house. At that point tell them, "I have to order a part." Come back next week and repeat the process all over again.

HOUSE SITTER

Your employer is out of town and, therefore, can't check up on you. They are paying you to feed the pets and collect the mail. Do what

"I gotta go back to the shop for a part. Shouldn't be gone more'n a coupla hours."

they're paying you for. Just do it on the day before they come home. Chances are, Kitty won't be real finicky.

VENTRILOQUIST

Inform the audience that your puppet is a deaf-mute. Not only do you look good for hiring the handicapped, but you're getting all the laughs. And since he doesn't speak, you don't have to waste time learning to talk without moving your lips.

TICKET TAKER

You are trying to get thousands of people into the building quickly. Don't bother checking to see if you gave them the half with the seat assignment on it. Hey, they're in the building. If they really want to see the game, they can watch it standing up.

WEATHERMAN

People make jokes about how often weathermen are wrong, and these trained professionals are putting a lot of time and effort into their predictions.

Time and effort are your enemies. Just guess. Your success rate will probably be the same. And the time you'll save on research can be put to better use playing Texas hold 'em online.

HOTEL HOUSEKEEPER

You can turn more rooms than anyone else if you don't hassle with little details like changing sheets or towels. And feel free to steal a lifetime supply of little soaps, shampoo, body lotion, pens, pads, glasses, and Bibles. Management will just assume guests took them.

FINANCIAL PLANNER

Let the crowd chase stocks, bonds, and real estate. Put your clients in commemorative plates. They'll thank you as they spend their golden years gliding down easy street, thanks to the Legends of NASCAR series.

DOMINATRIX

Don't try to hurt anyone.

EMBALMER

One of the keys to running a good business is cutting costs, and I would bet embalming fluid is much more expensive than, say, tap water.

LAWYER

Just be honest. There is no better way than that to really stink at being a lawyer.

ELECTRICIAN

Show up at the job site with Don King hair. If your client asks for references, simply say, "None of them are living."

TAXI DRIVER

Make sure the inside of your cab smells like a combination of the dumpster behind the fish house and incense. Invent a language and stick to it. Jackrabbit starts and stops and horn honking are also a nice touch.

"My client has a long history of bad decisions. If he
didn't do this, I'll kiss a monkey's butt on Main Street,
but that decision ultimately lies in your hands."

TIP: Hang an air freshener from the rearview mirror, but only after marinating it in a mixture of cat urine, sulfur, and blue cheese for about ten days.

FEMALE RUNWAY MODEL

Eat a cheeseburger. That's all. Seriously, if you eat a cheeseburger you will look so fat next to the other models that you will probably be modeling maternity clothes before the end of the week.

SPERM DONOR

Show up with a bucket.

ASTRONAUT

If you are an astronaut, you have billions of dollars of research behind you as you carry out the

"I'll be back tomorrow."

dreams of the most brilliant scientists on earth. With that in mind, here are a few things NASA might not want to hear you say as you travel through deep space:

- "Where am I going again?"
- "We accidentally just shot all of our food out the hatch. How important is it that we bring everybody back?"
- "Houston, request permission to do a couple of doughnuts. Let's see what this hot rod's got!"
- "I suspect an alien took over Jerry's body. How do we kill it without killing Jerry?"
- "Okay, who's up for a game of water balloons?"
- "Your last transmission was garbled, but I think you said, 'Head straight for the sun.'"

MARRIAGE COUNSELOR

Couples who attend marriage counseling are looking for an unbiased third party. But that

"Look, guys, I snuck my dog in!"

would require actually listening to their problems, and that is exhausting.

Think about it: If you solve all their problems, you're not only working too hard, you're going to be out a client you could easily string along for years—and that's bad for the bottom line. Here are some things you can "throw out there" to keep them coming back:

- "When she says she's going to the grocery store, are you sure that's where she's really going?"
- "Do you find any of her friends attractive?"
- "Maybe she doesn't listen because she's distracted by your receding hairline?"
- "Do you have money put away that your spouse doesn't know about?"
- "So you feel confident when he's out of town that he's not hooking up with someone who's much more attractive than you?"
- "Perhaps you don't have the necessary equipment to satisfy her."

"If you could change ten things about your spouse,
what would they be?"

BUTCHER

Become a vegetarian. A real militant one. Sell the customers meat, but make them feel horribly guilty about eating it. Post signs around the shop that say things like "Chickens are people too" and "Select from our wide range of murder victims for your dining pleasure."

GROCERY BAGGER

Do you really want to bag groceries for the rest of your life? Of course not! There's nowhere to take a nap in the front of the store. If you do the job poorly enough, they'll probably find something else for you to do, like work in the back. Which is where all the good napping hidey-holes are.

With that in mind, here are some examples of what might go in what bags in what order:

Bag #1: eggs, tomatoes, twelve-pack of beer

Bag #2: grapes, marshmallows, ten-pound bag of sugar

Bag #3: newspaper, ice cream, hot rotisserie chicken

Bag #4: bottle of spaghetti sauce, bread, large canned goods

Bag #5: Styrofoam container of soup, steak knives

TRAFFIC COP

Let's face it: Standing in the middle of a street when the traffic lights are broken is dangerous. So stay on the sidewalk and direct traffic from there.

Sure, a lot of drivers won't see you, and those who will probably won't have any idea what you're trying to tell them to do, but you'll be safe. And that's what's really important.

CHEERLEADER

Cheerleaders are fun to watch and bring a great energy to a game, but when it's the fourth quarter and the home team is getting routed, optimistic cheering just becomes annoying.

You are leading the crowd, so accurately reflect what they are feeling. At the very least you should be mad and depressed, like everybody in the stands. A few of you should throw down your pom-poms and just leave.

Change your cheers to reflect what is really happening, such as: "Watch them gag / watch them choke / cheering for you / is a joke! Goooooo %&#@ yourselves!"

DEMOLITIONIST

Not always properly jotting down important details like addresses is a great way to stink at this job.

POLITICIAN

Just keep doing what you all are doing. It stinks big-time as it is.

DENTIST

Have lots of hard candies and jawbreakers in dishes all over your office. Hand out lollipops to all the kids who have good checkups.

"Sez here we're supposed to be at 138 <u>NORTH</u> Hampton Street."

DOG BREEDER

Don't get hung up on details like bloodlines or even breeds. Let the dogs decide whom they'd like to mate with. Any kind of puppy is cute, and it's not like a customer is going to bring them back when they grow up. They're already attached and you've long since cashed the check.

SCIENTIST

How do you stink at being a scientist? Build a Frankenstein monster! That never goes well.

You set out innocently enough—just your average genius wanting to create a new life from dead body parts. But somewhere along the line it always goes wrong. You start to get a little obsessed. It begins to affect your day-to-day life.

Not to mention that the monster always winds up killing people, and then everybody ends up being mad at you.

So if you are presently spending your time and energy searching for medical break-

throughs and ways to push mankind forward—fine. Do what you gotta do. But in your spare time, try pickin' up a shovel and headin' out to the nearest graveyard.

MEDICAL EXAMINER

How could you possibly stink at this job? I'll tell you how. Don't bother checking who anybody is before you start cutting. Any motionless person will do. The inevitable screwups will create stories people are going to talk about for years to come.

And no matter how a person you're examining passed away, *always* determine the cause of death to be murder. Then sign the death certificate "Quincy."

HAIRDRESSER

This is another job where customers can ruin your day. Sure, these people keep the business going and provide money for you to pay your rent and buy groceries. But if you don't own the business, they can really cut into your vacantly-staring-off-into-space time.

There are a lot of repeat customers, and if you're too good, you are going to be super stressed trying to work everybody in. That is why it is necessary to continually "thin the herd."

You will have demanding and annoying clients, but rest assured that in one session you can "cut" them loose. Simply do the opposite of what they ask for. If they want to leave it long, go with the buzz cut. If they want to keep it blond, make them Goth. There may be a few tears and curse words, but hair grows back out eventually, and your calendar will never be full.

SECURITY GUARD

Nap time has never been easier since they came out with glasses with eyeballs painted on the lenses. Never, ever investigate anything suspicious. That's being nosy, and being nosy isn't nice. Besides, if someone is up to no good, you could get hurt in the confrontation, and then you might miss work.

After all, you are unarmed and it's not your stuff you are guarding. And remember, nobody's going to come to help you when they hear you say over your walkie-talkie, "He's got a gun!"

REAL ESTATE AGENT

As a professional with access to someone else's home, you are entrusted with a great responsibility. On the other hand, empty homes owned by other people make great party houses.

There's nothing quite like the face of a po-

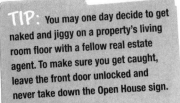

TIP: You may one day decide to get naked and jiggy on a property's living room floor with a fellow real estate agent. To make sure you get caught, leave the front door unlocked and never take down the Open House sign.

"They got the drop on me. But as soon as I change
my shorts I think I can take 'em down."

tential buyer walking through a house that looks like a dumpster vomited, led by a real estate agent who smells like a liquor store. This, along with keeping the price high and your effort low, could keep this house on the market for years to come.

TEACHER

Teaching is hard. Hanging out isn't. So if you really want to avoid the hard part and stink at teaching, become friends with all your students. Give out A's like a skunk gives out odor. The students and parents will love you! You,

TIP: As a homework assignment, demand that your students sit on the couch and watch television.

my friend, will always be at the top of the "favorite teacher" poll and will have a job for life.

Today's Curriculum:

History: Who are your favorite bands from last year?

Math: How many hours a week do you spend playing video games?

Science: What are the ingredients of Red Bull?

English: Use the word "random" in a sentence.

Geography: Where do you like to hang out?

JANITOR

Wire the principal's intercom system so that it is on all the time. At some point she will say something that should not be broadcast, which will create a controversy that everyone will be talking about. That will take all the attention off you, and that means you can read the latest *National Enquirer* in peace.

PERSONAL TRAINER

You are the trainer, not the one who needs to get in shape, so you want to get through the day without doing any physical activity. Never show a client how to do an exercise; just describe it. Even if you have to say, "Wrong!" twenty times, don't pick up a barbell or get on a machine. Don't even bend your legs unless it's to put your coffee or your magazine down.

Take advantage of the fact that simply by being there your client is admitting that he's out of shape and needs your help. It's perfectly okay to say incredibly insulting things under the guise that it's part of the workout routine.

OPTOMETRIST

Place your chart six feet farther away than it should be. As an inside joke, have the chart read:

```
I  A  M  B  L
I  N  D  A  S
A  B  A  T  I
N  E  E  D  T
H  I  S  D  O
C  T  O  R
```

Trust me. You'll have your customers for life, and all you have to do is keep giving them slightly stronger glasses every time they come in.

TIP: You can also smear the chart with Vaseline just to amplify your customers' need for your services.

OTORHINOLARYNGOLOGIST

You definitely had the right idea picking this as a profession. Nobody can pronounce your occupation. And nobody knows what it is you do, so you can make it up as you go along.

DOOR-TO-DOOR SALESPERSON

In sales they say, don't take NO for an answer. For most people this means the hard sell. For the purposes of this book and helping you stink at your job, I'm saying, *Never* take no for an answer. No matter how many times someone says he doesn't want to buy your vacuum cleaner, keep pitching.

Even while you are being physically carried out of an angry customer's house by law enforcement, keep pitching how great the vacuum cleaner is. Show up at his workplace and start vacuuming and pitching. Follow him to restaurants and movie theaters and vacuum.

If that doesn't work, run an ad in the newspaper aimed at your potential customer, telling him why he should buy your vacuum cleaner. If *that* doesn't work, rent a billboard. Don't rule out skywriting.

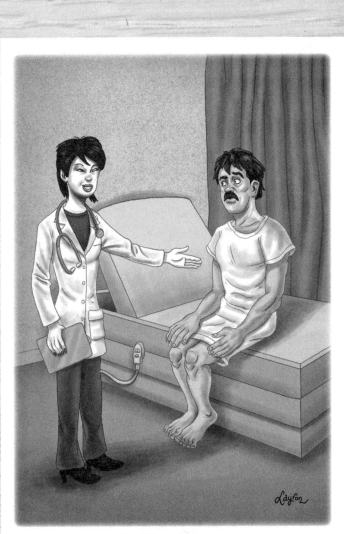

"Mr. Hillcrest, I'm your
othrhyfodimpeejucklehensoohiyshelipplongyrumsarairhimposiologist.
Have you had any pain in your armpit, throat, or thigh?"

If the answer is still no, call him up and pretend you are a DJ and say he has won two tickets to a Tim McGraw concert. Then write a song about how the customer should buy your vacuum cleaner, somehow get in touch with Tim McGraw, pay him to learn your song, and get him to play it at the concert.

If you're still hearing "No," buy a house that is for sale on the customer's street and get a doctor to live in it. Then fake your own death by paying a scientist to come up with a pill that safely slows your heart rate and breathing to the point where you appear to be dead. Take the pill and wait in the potential customer's driveway.

When he pulls in, throw yourself in front of his car so that it hits you real hard. (It has to look authentic! So beforehand, hire a stunt-person to teach you how to take the hit.) As you lie there, have the doctor from down the street run over, check your vital signs, and say you are not going to make it.

This is the point where you whisper that your last wish is for the customer to buy your vacuum cleaner. When he says, "Yes," make sure it's clear—no refunds! The doctor can then take you away to the hospital.

Once the sale goes through, you don't want the customer to know that you are actually alive, so get plastic surgery and legally change your name. Eight years later, go back and sell him a new vacuum cleaner.

IN CONCLUSION

Dear Reader,

If, in the future, our paths cross and I hire you to work for me, please ignore everything you just read.

ABOUT THE AUTHORS

JEFF FOXWORTHY is the largest-selling comedy-recording artist in history, a multiple Grammy Award nominee, and the bestselling author of more than twenty-five books, including his Redneck Dictionaries. He is the host of the Fox television series *Are You Smarter Than a 5th Grader?* Jeff also starred in all three *Blue Collar Comedy Tour* movies, which have sold more than eight million copies and are some of the highest-rated movies in Comedy Central history. His syndicated weekly radio show, *The Foxworthy Countdown,* is carried in more than 220 markets across the United States. A Georgia native, he lives with his wife and their two daughters in Atlanta.

BRIAN HARTT is a veteran writer and producer of hit comedies, including *The Kids in the Hall, MADtv,* and *The Jamie Kennedy Experiment.* He also worked with Jeff on *Blue Collar TV.* He lives in Los Angeles with his wife and their two children.

ABOUT THE TYPE

This book was set in Adobe Caslon. William Caslon released his first typefaces in 1722. His types were based on seventeenth-century Dutch old style designs, which were then used extensively in England. Because of their incredible practicality Caslon's designs met with instant success. Caslon's types became popular throughout Europe and the American colonies; printer Benjamin Franklin hardly used any other typeface. The first printings of the American Declaration of Independence and the Constitution were set in Caslon. For her Caslon revival, designer Carol Twombly studied specimen pages printed by William Caslon between 1734 and 1770. Ideally suited for text, Adobe Caslon is right for magazines, journals, book publishing, and corporate communications.